I'M ALLERGIC

I'M ALLERGIC TO WHEAT

By Maria Nelson

Gareth Stevens
PUBLISHING

Please visit our website, www.garethstevens.com. For a free color catalog of all our high-quality books, call toll free 1-800-542-2595 or fax 1-877-542-2596.

Library of Congress Cataloging-in-Publication Data

Nelson, Maria.
I'm allergic to wheat / by Maria Nelson.
p. cm. — (I'm allergic)
Includes index.
ISBN 978-1-4824-0990-1 (pbk.)
ISBN 978-1-4824-0991-8 (6-pack)
ISBN 978-1-4824-0989-5 (library binding)
1. Food allergy in children — Juvenile literature. 2. Wheat — Juvenile literature. I. Nelson, Maria. II. Title.
RJ386.5 N45 2014
618.92—d23

Published in 2015 by
Gareth Stevens Publishing
111 East 14th Street, Suite 349
New York, NY 10003

Copyright © 2015 Gareth Stevens Publishing

Designer: Nicholas Domiano
Editor: Kristen Rajczak

Photo credits: Cover, pp. 1, 15 iStock/Thinkstock.com; pp. 3–24 (background texture) Michel Borges/Shutterstock.com; p. 5 BestPhotoStudio/Shutterstock.com; p. 7 Jacek Chabraszewski/Shutterstock.com; p. 9 bikeriderlondon/Shutterstock.com; p. 11 © iStockphoto.com/Kuligssen; p. 13 Intropin/Wikimedia Commons; p. 17 Peter Dazeley/ The Image Bank/Getty Images; p. 19 R. Nelson/Flickr/Getty Images; p. 21 Daniel Acker/ Bloomberg via Getty Images.

Printed in the United States of America

CPSIA compliance information: Batch #CS15GS: For further information contact Gareth Stevens, New York, New York at 1-800-542-2595.

Contents

Boldface words appear in the glossary.

A Common Allergy

If someone in your family has an **allergy**, you're more likely to have one. Some people have allergic **reactions** to certain foods. Wheat is one of the most common food allergies in children. Luckily, many children outgrow it!

Protein Problem

An allergic reaction happens when someone with a wheat allergy eats wheat products. The body **identifies** a **protein** in the wheat as harmful. It creates special parts of the blood called antibodies to fight it.

Reacting

An allergic reaction starts a few minutes to a few hours after eating something containing wheat. Reactions include an itchy feeling in the mouth or throat. Some people might have a stuffy nose and watery eyes.

9

Raised, itchy patches of skin called hives may also appear after eating wheat. The worst allergic reaction is called anaphylaxis (aa-nuh-fuh-LAK-suhs). It may include a tight feeling in the chest and throat, trouble breathing, and passing out.

Best to Stay Away

Anaphylaxis and other bad reactions can be treated by a shot of a drug called epinephrine (eh-puh-NEH-fruhn). However, there's only one good way to control a wheat allergy. Stay away from foods containing wheat!

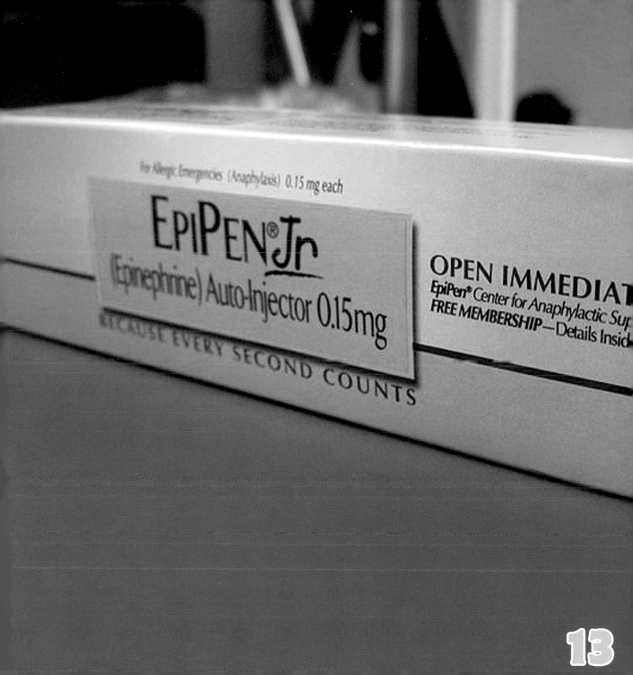

For Allergic Emergencies (Anaphylaxis) 0.15 mg each

EpiPen®Jr
(Epinephrine) Auto-Injector 0.15mg
BECAUSE EVERY SECOND COUNTS

OPEN IMMEDIAT
EpiPen® Center for Anaphylactic Sup
FREE MEMBERSHIP—Details Inside

13

Don't Eat It!

Baked goods such as cookies and cake are often made with wheat flour. Pasta, breakfast cereals, and bread are, too. If you have a wheat allergy, it's best if you don't eat any of these.

15

Surprisingly, ketchup, ice cream, and potato chips could contain wheat! Check if a food is made with wheat. The label will say so. Be careful of products that could have been produced near wheat. They can cause allergic reactions, too!

Other Grains

Grains such as barley, oats, and rye contain similar proteins to those in wheat. So, some people with wheat allergies are allergic to them as well. If you're not, these grains are a great **substitute** for wheat.

Celiac Disease

One of the four wheat proteins that cause an allergic reaction is gluten. Gluten is the protein that causes people with celiac **disease** to get sick. Celiac disease isn't a food allergy and causes different problems than wheat allergies.

NET WT 20 OZ (1 LB 4 OZ)

This stone ground whole grain cornmeal makes cornbread with a superb flavor and texture. This medium grind, gluten free cornmeal also works well for breading and creates delightfully crunchy cornmeal pancakes.

NET WT 24 OZ (1 LB 8 OZ) 680g

3.59
Cost Per Unit 18¢

GLUTEN FREE

GLUTEN FREE

Glossary

allergy: a body's sensitivity to usually harmless things in the surroundings, such as dust, pollen, or foods

disease: illness

identify: recognize

protein: one of the building blocks of food

reaction: response

substitute: something that takes the place of something else

For More Information

Books

Robbins, Lynette. *How to Deal with Allergies*. New York, NY: PowerKids Press, 2010.

Tuminelly, Nancy. *Cool Wheat-Free Recipes: Delicious & Fun Foods Without Gluten*. Minneapolis, MN: ABDO Publishing Company, 2013.

Websites

Gluten-Free Kids Recipes
www.celiaccentral.org/kids/recipes/
These recipes don't use wheat products or products that have been processed with wheat and are safe for those with wheat allergies.

Wheat Allergy
kidshealth.org/parent/medical/allergies/ wheat_allergy.html
Read more about having a wheat allergy and how to live with it.

Publisher's note to educators and parents: Our editors have carefully reviewed these websites to ensure that they are suitable for students. Many websites change frequently, however, and we cannot guarantee that a site's future contents will continue to meet our high standards of quality and educational value. Be advised that students should be closely supervised whenever they access the Internet.

Index